The Best Way for Veterans to Land a Federal Job

How to get Military Veterans Preference

Simple Steps to ensure you get the Military Veterans' Preference eligibility you earned.

Written By RJ Leblanc MBA

Published by VetPref Staffing Consultants LLC

www.vetpref.com

http://on.fb.me/1ATDOth

@vetpref

Legal Disclaimer

Dedication

"From this day to the ending of the world, But we in it shall be remembered-We few, we happy few, we band of brothers; for he today that sheds his blood with me shall be my brother" **William Shakespeare**

This book is dedicated to all the men and women past, present, and future, who get up every morning, without question, don their uniforms, strap on their equipment, and head out the door to risk life and limb defending this great nation for God, Country, and Family! Yours and Mine. Thank you!

Table of Contents

Why I Wrote This Book..5

Why You Should Read This Book.........................7

Vernacular...9

A Few Words about Federal Hiring.....................11

The History of Veteran's Preference....................19

What is Veterans' Preference?.............................28

When does Veterans Preference Apply?.............33

Types of Veterans' Preference.............................35

Special Hiring Authorities for Veterans...............42

What to Look For on Your DD Form 214...............47

Navigating USA Jobs..55

Afterword...63

Definitions for Common Terms Used in Vacancy
Announcements..64

Resource Links...69

Why I Wrote This Book

I have been where you are. I retired from the Military in 2006. I tried to quit working but my wife wouldn't let me. I stayed home for a couple of months until I drove her crazy and she threatened to put me out of the house. I started applying to everything under the sun. I even got a few interviews but most were for jobs that took time to build the pay and benefits I was looking for. I also began apply to Federal Jobs. I knew what I wanted. I was looking to continue that guaranteed salary my recruiter told me about so many years ago. The knowledge that on the 1st and the 15th you can count on a paycheck is very comforting. You don't get that with most civilian jobs. Now that I am retired I metaphorically go out and salute the mailbox once a month and grab my check. The 20 years was worth it!

Before I retired I went to all of the Transition Assistance Programs they offer or make mandatory. You know the ones, ACAP, TAP, etc. and the rest of the boxes they make you check before anyone will sign off on your clearing papers. As many of you can probably relate, the classes were not that great (at least back then) and I found myself drifting off and thinking about my retirement in the sun. Luckily, I was in Recruiting and Retention for a long time so I knew my way around a DD Form 214 and understood many of the terms and acronyms used in most federal vacancy announcements. Even with that knowledge, it still took three years before I secured a Federal Job. There are some specific reasons it took that long, all of them my fault. That is a subject for another book.

Within a couple of months I found a recruiting job that wasn't commission based and settled in. It didn't take long to figure out I was not in the right place. I continued to apply to federal jobs. Like I said it took me three years but after many frustrating attempts, I was finally hired as a Human Resources Specialist which is a fancy name for the person who reviews your application, and resume. In federal hiring, a Human Resources Specialist reviews your qualifications, determines your Veterans' Preference, and adds your name to a list of eligible candidates for the Selecting Official's/Hiring Manager's consideration.

I have reviewed thousands of applications and resumes. I often get angry at what I see. I see resumes that are incomplete or full of fluff and buff and no way related to the position you are applying to or email address that are inappropriate etc. I think to myself, what are they teaching you people out there? It pains me to disqualify or not refer a Veteran but I have to do it every day.

That is why I decided to do something about it. I was so frustrated with what I was seeing I even created the blog site VetPref (http://vetpref.com) where Veterans can get free help with applications and resumes. I post articles related to Veterans employment, resumes interviewing tips, and general insight on getting hired. Veterans like you and me who want to secure a job with the Federal Government can do so easily if you educate yourself and understand the process. This eBook is part of that. Working for the Federal Government has been a blessing for me. If you use this book, it can be for you!

Why You Should Read This Book

*"Whoever said the pen is mightier than the sword
obviously never encountered automatic weapons".*
Douglas MacArthur

I think it is reasonable for me to assume you bought this book because you are trying secure a job with the federal government. The most important part of the federal hiring process is getting your name on a Certificate/Referral list. This is the list of people that Human Resources Specialist gives to the Selecting Official/Hiring Manager to choose the person they want to hire. Everyone on the list is qualified for the position. The list is usually in alphabetical order except for the Veterans. Veterans are listed at the top of the list. Here is a simple scenario. A Selecting official is given a Certificate/Referral list with 25 names on it. All 25 of these candidates are fully qualified for the position. There are two Veterans on the list. If one of those Veterans is you, you have just cut your competition from 24 other candidates to only one other person, the Veteran. If you are the <u>only</u> Veteran on the list, the competition is over. The hiring manager must offer the position to you before any Non-Veteran on the list. I will talk more about this later.

Knowing and understanding the preference eligibilities that will float your name to the top of the Certificate/Referral list is the most important part of the application process for a Veteran. This is a small but extremely important piece of the application puzzle. Your name at the top of the competitive Certificate/Referral list guarantees you must be considered before all non-preference eligible candidates when a Hiring Manager is trying to fill a position.

I want readers to know you can find virtually everything you will read in this book free on the Internet if you know where to look. Finding information on Veterans' Preference is the easy part. The hard part is figuring out what to do with all the information once you find it! You could spend hours trying to make heads or tails out of the unfamiliar laws, regulations, terms, acronyms, you come across. Then and most importantly, you have to spend hours trying figure out how to utilize that information when you are applying for federal jobs.

This book will show you how to secure the Veterans' Preference eligibilities you have earned and rightly deserve. Whether you are about to be released from active duty, retired Military, or you have been out for a while, this book will help guide you through the Veterans' Preference eligibilities piece of the application process. This is information especially helpful if you separated from the Military a while ago. I will discuss the federal hiring process, the important parts of your DD214, and I will walk you through the section of USA Jobs where Veterans' Preference is claimed. The reason you should read this book is simple. Having all this information in one place and explaining it in terms that are easy to understand, will be a tremendous advantage to you when applying to federal jobs. Having that advantage is what gives this book its value.

Vernacular

The dumbest private in the room. Many of us have had Non-Commissioned Officers in our Military careers give us sound advice. After all NCO's are the backbone of the Military right? One of my mentors, a Senior NCO, gave me some advice one day while I was preparing for a class to give to my platoon. I was a young E-5 Buck Sargent with no clue. Not quite as bad as a butter bar 2nd Lieutenant (sorry couldn't resist) but close. I had the regulations out, had examples of things, etc. I thought I was going to impress everyone and be smarter than everybody in the room. He looked at me and said, *"Sarge what the **** are you doing"?* I was kind of taken aback because after all I had spent many hours putting this together the perfect PowerPoint presentation and I was pretty proud of it. I asked him what he meant. He said when you give a class you have to present to the *"dumbest private in the room"*.

It took me a second but I figured out what he was saying. He wasn't making a disparaging comment about some of our, shall we say "intellectually challenged" soldiers, you know the ones. He was saying know and understand your audience. So I thought back to when I was the dumbest private in the room and couldn't make heads or tails out of what my Sargent was saying and was dying a slow death by PowerPoint. So I revamped my class.by making it clearer and more concise. It was a great success! I got complimented by my Platoon Leader and the Company Commander as well as the dumbest privates in the room. The reason I reminisce about the knowledge imparted from my mentor is because that is how I approached writing this book. Most of us Veterans are down to earth, no nonsense, tell-it like it is kind of people. We believe in BLUF; the Bottom Line Up Front. I use that same style when explaining topics in the book. I try to give you the reader what the "official" laws, policies, and regulations say, but then give you the "straight skinny" on what all this stuff means. Some of it is opinion and some of it is based on my experience. I like to have things explained down as far as possible. I think most of us are like that. If I think someone is going to ask a question about a term or word I will try to answer the question before it is asked. I will apologize in advance if my manner of speech seems dumbed down or elementary.

A Few Words about Federal Hiring

"If you put the federal government in charge of the Sahara Desert, in 5 years there'd be a shortage of sand"—Milton Friedman

When I first started applying to federal jobs, I completed the Veterans' Preference portion of my applications correctly. The Veterans' Preference portion is only one variable in the equation. I would get frustrated at the fact that I was not called for an interview or just never heard anything back. I would get emails from USAJobs (http://usajobs.gov) stating that I passed basic qualifications and been referred to the hiring official. I am thinking awesome right? Then I heard nothing. And forget about trying to reach anyone at the agency's servicing human resources center. I did not understand how preference eligibilities, qualifications, and referral systems, worked on the hiring/staffing side of the process. To be hired you must overcome two main hurdles. First, the Human Resources Specialist/Staffing Specialist who reviews your application must refer you to the Selecting Official/Hiring Manager, and second, the selecting official must select you. A common misconception among Veterans is that Veterans' Preference guarantees you a job or it means that an agency has to hire you over everyone else. That is only partially true. The truth is that a Selecting Official/Hiring Manager does not have to hire you just because you are a Veteran even if you are disabled or use alternate hiring authorities like VRA or VEOA (more on that later). The only thing the selecting official must do is **consider** you over all other **NON-Preference** eligible candidates with all things being **equal**. In other words, if the selecting official is looking at two individuals who are qualified for the position and one of them is a Veteran, they must choose the Veteran. They must consider you **provided** you are otherwise **qualified for the position** and have been referred by the Human Resources Specialist. That is the sticky part. You have to make sure through your application and resume that the Human Resources Specialist has no choice but to refer you because you have articulated the required specialized experience for the position. Keep in mind, the Human Resources Specialist does not have to refer you if they think you are not qualified. The selecting official can also decide not to hire anyone if he or she does not like the candidate pool.

You must always remember that if you are applying from outside the federal government (no... Military time does not count as federal government time for this purpose) you are in a competition for the position you are applying too. You are competing with everyone else who applied both Veteran and non-Veteran. I remember the first interview I had. It was for a GS-05 position. I sat in front of a panel of three people. After getting to know each other, I learned that two of the three were Veterans. I thought I had the job locked! After the interview, I asked when I could except to hear from them. One of the panel members said, "Well it may take a while." I said, "But I have Veterans' Preference." He said, "Well we have 25 other Veterans to look at so it may be a few weeks." Later I received an email for USAJobs stating I was not selected for the position.

That shattered the perception I had about Veterans' Preference. I thought my Veterans' Preference would guarantee me the job. I was naïve in my thinking. For some reason it did not occur to me that there were many other Veterans applying for jobs. I may have had Veterans' Preference but so did the other 25 folks they were going to interview! What a "duh" moment for me. Human Resources Specialists only evaluate what you the applicant presents for review. They cannot make assumptions. It is your responsibility to articulate your knowledge, skills and abilities for the position you are applying to in your resume. They cannot and should not try to make something out of nothing. A prime example is when a Veteran claims preference and does not attach any supporting documents. The result is that you are likely to be referred if you are qualified, but not as a Veteran with preference. The rules for supporting documentation can differ from agency to agency. That is because The Office of Personnel Management (OPM) (http://1.usa.gov/1xqsK5k) leaves some decisions about preference validation to the individual agency. In some agencies if you do not provide supporting documentation, you do not get preference. The best rule of thumb to follow is – if you claim it, support it with the proper documentation. This includes college transcripts. If you are going to use college transcripts in your resume (I always do), take the time to get an official copy. Official not in the sense that they are sealed, but a good legible copy you can scan in to your USA Jobs profile.

As a Human Resources Specialist, I can't stand to try to decipher some blurry internet copy of your class schedule. Just don't do it. You may be required later to send in a sealed copy but not at the application phase. Supporting documentation may mean the difference between you getting referred and not. **READ** the Vacancy Announcement in its entirety. It will tell you everything you need to know.

I will add one more thing about qualifications. Just because **YOU** think you are qualified for a position does not mean that you are. Human Resource Specialists have a set of guidelines they must use when determining qualifications. The Office of Personnel Management (OPM) sets the qualification standards. You have to get through the Human Resources Specialist before you get to the Selecting Official/Hiring Manager. Read the vacancy announcement thoroughly. Review the required qualifications. Ensure your resume supports your qualifications. Qualifications can be subjective when the Human Resources Specialist is trying to match your previous job duties to the skills required for the position. Do not force the Human Resources Specialist to make the leap between your resume and the required skills for the position. Use your resume to build a bridge to the required qualifications from the vacancy announcement.

Many times the Human Resources Specialist has no Military background. If you use Military acronyms and terms, only an Infantryman would understand, the Human Resources Specialist is less likely to see the qualification picture you are trying to paint. In my opinion, when writing federal resumes, more is better. The majority of Federal jobs base qualifications on how much specialized experience you have not education. OPM defines specialized experience as *"Experience that equipped the applicant with the particular knowledge, skills, and abilities (KSA's) to perform successfully the duties of the position, and that is typically in or related to the position to be filled. To be creditable, specialized experience must have been equivalent to at least the next lower grade level.* It is crucial that you understand that definition. In some cases, a requirement exists for certain classes or degree program and in other cases, education can substitute for specialized experience.

How do I know if I am qualified before I apply? A good rule of thumb to use is, if you have never done the duties (either exact or equivalent) in the required qualifications section of the Vacancy Announcement, you are likely not qualified for the position with specialized experience. See the below experience requirement for a Medical Services Assistant (MSA) at the Veterans' Administration at the GS-05 level. Go to the OPM Pay and Leave (http://1.usa.gov/13X1XDp) webpage to understand the different Federal Pay Schedules.

QUALIFICATIONS REQUIRED:

Back to top

BASIC REQUIREMENTS.

Citizenship: Citizen of the United States.

Certification: None required.

GS-5 MSA (Full Performance Level)

This job is at the GS 5 level. Full Performance Level means that this the highest pay grade this position has. You would have to compete again for a different position with a higher pay grade.

Experience or Education: One year of specialized experience or 4 years of education above high school.

Assignment: This is the full performance level for MSAs. At this level, the MSA performs a full range of duties. The MSA is responsible for scheduling appointments, including interpreting and verifying provider orders in accordance with VHA national scheduling guidelines. Assignments at this level include, but are not limited to: scheduling, ca... ...er consults; entering no-show information; monitor... ...itoring both inpatient and outpatient appointme... ...e completed in order to obtain appropriate work... ...ance information; processing all emergency... ...e hospitals; performing basic eligibil... ...verage (i.e., TRICARE, sharing agreements, ...c.).

These KSA's are at the GS-4 Level. 1 year Specialized Experience at the next lower grade. You have to demonstrate in your resume you have done these duties.

Demonstrated Knowledge, Skills, and Abilities. Candidates must demonstrate the KSAs below:

1. Ability to operate computerized programs and databases in order to enter, modify and retrieve sensitive information/data into or from electronic medical records, scheduling systems and/or reports.
2. Knowledge of basic medical terminology.
3. Ability to make appointments in a clinical setting.
4. Ability to work independently in the accomplishment of a wide variety of duties, including setting priorities and coordinating work.
5. Ability to communicate effectively and professionally with employees at varying grade levels.
6. Ability to identify customer's concerns, perform the tasks required to resolve the issue accurately and timely, and follow-up as necessary to ensure a satisfactory resolution.

The Salary Range for the position above is $31,628 to $41,122 per year. It is likely that you will start at the low end if you have never worked for the Federal Government before. The low end in this case would be GS-05 STEP 1 and the high end would be GS-05 STEP 10. You get incremental STEP increases over time. If someone were to apply to this position and they were already a GS-05 STEP 4, then the salary would be somewhere in between. Don't apply to positions based on salary. Typically an E-7 before they retire, is making about $65,000 a year with salary, rations, housing, and medical benefits included. That is roughly the equivalent of a GS-11 Step 4. Unless you have experience directly related to that position at the grade level below, you are likely not qualified. This may sound confusing but the Specialize Experience you see in the Vacancy Announcement is at the next lower grade level than the one you are applying to. Reread the definition of Specialized Experience above. It says at least one year at the next lower grade. Don't waste your time applying. I know that sounds harsh but it is true. Again, make sure you read the announcement thoroughly. Everything you need to know about the job duties and requirements for the position is in the vacancy announcement. In preparation for applying, take a moment and sit and think about all the things you have done in your military career. It is likely you have done some of the duties listed but you know them by another name. Use your resume to tell a story about yourself that will leave no doubt in the Human Resources Specialist's mind that you are a well-qualified candidate and why they should refer you to the Selecting Official/Hiring Manager.

You say "but I have a degree". The following table from the OPM website shows the amounts of education and/or experience required to qualify for positions covered by the Administrative and Management Positions Qualifications Standard. As you can see to qualify with education alone, at the GS-11 level, mentioned above you would need a Ph. D. or equivalent doctoral degree. In my opinion, degrees are nice to have but for federal hiring they are not always necessary. Do not disqualify yourself from a position because you don't have a degree. In federal hiring Specialized Experience carries more weight in the majority of jobs. There are exceptions of course like, nurses, doctors, biologists, engineers, or other positions that require professional degrees or credentials.

GRADE	EDUCATION	EXPERIENCE	
		GENERAL	SPECIALIZED
GS-5	4-year course of study leading to a bachelor's degree	3 years. 1 year of which was equivalent to at least GS-4	None
GS-7	1 full year of graduate level education *or* superior academic achievement	None	1 year equivalent to at least GS-5
GS-9	master's or equivalent graduate degree *or* 2 full years of progressively higher level graduate education leading to such a degree *or* LL.B. or J.D.. if related	None	1 year equivalent to at least GS-7
GS-11	Ph.D. or equivalent doctoral degree *or* 3 full years of progressively higher level graduate education leading to such a degree *or* LL.M.. if related	None	1 year equivalent to at least GS-9
GS-12 and above	None	None	1 year equivalent to at least next lower grade level

Another thing most Veterans do not understand is that the hiring process takes time. You must have patience. On May 11, 2011, The President issued a Presidential Memorandum (http://1.usa.gov/1D1wcFq) called Improving the Federal Recruitment and Hiring Process. The target audience was for the Heads of Executive Departments and Agencies. The initial paragraph says, *"to deliver the quality services and results to the American people expect and deserve, the Federal Government must recruit highly qualified employees, and public service should be a career of choice for the most talented Americans. Yet the complexity and inefficiency of today's Federal Hiring process deters many highly qualified individuals from seeking and obtaining jobs in the Federal government."* This memorandum instructed OPM to develop a way to make the hiring process more efficient.

The OPM recommendation is for an 80-day hiring model. That means it should take 80 days from the time the selecting official submits a request for a vacancy announcement to the day you show up for work. You say to yourself 80 days is a long time and if you are looking for a job and you are correct. Believe me this is a step up from what it was.

There are many factors involved in the hiring process that lend themselves to why it takes that long to hire someone including the length of time the vacancy is open, the number of candidates in the applicant pool, or how long the hiring manger takes to make a selection etc. For example if a vacancy announcement is open for 14 days that leaves 66 days. If there are 100 applicants in the applicant pool it may take another two weeks for the Human Resources Specialist to qualify all 100. It could take even longer if there are multiple grades advertised. Now we have 52 days, and so on. Bottom line with federal hiring is you have to be patient.

The History of Veterans' Preference

*"Take care for him who shall have borne the battle and
for his widow and his orphan"~ Abraham Lincoln*

Why does the United States Government give Veterans' Preference in hiring to those who chose to serve their country? The short answer is to reward Veterans for their service. America, her people, and by default her government recognize your sacrifices. President Theodore Roosevelt said, "Government jobs belong to the American people, not politicians and shall be filled only with regard to public service." I know what you are saying because I said it too. If Teddy could see things now. What happened? Federal hiring just is not that simple anymore. The long answer to the above question is a bit more complicated and plays out historically in legislation. The History of the Civil Service and Veterans' Preference is quite lengthy. I think it is important to understand where we come from to know where we are going. This will be a condensed version and I will start by discussing the beginnings of the Civil Service and move on to how Veterans' Preference came into existence up to its present form.

The result of the Revolutionary War was the creation of our country. From the first days of Republic, the government has been concerned that dedicated and hardworking citizens with good character be employed to carry out the business of the people. **The Constitution; (http://1.usa.gov/1vkr5u6)** (Article II, Section 2, paragraph 2) has provisions for hiring higher officials like, "Ambassadors, other public Ministers, and Consuls, Judges of the Supreme Court, and all other officers of the United States whose appointments are not herein otherwise provided for" shall be Presidential nomination and Senate, confirmed.

It is a little more ambiguous when it comes to appointing officers of lesser rank. Congress empowered the President, Courts of Law, or Heads of Departments to make these lessor appointments. Before any real legislation passed to help Veterans, certain Soldiers received rewards for their service. This early form of Preference based on the European model primarily offered rewards such as land, pensions, and bonuses for service, disability allowance, and hospitalization for injuries incurred while in uniform.

In the early years of the government, President George Washington (1789-1797) tried to hire men of character for employment with the Federal government. Honesty, efficiency, and adherence to the Constitution were of the utmost concern. President Washington selected men from all over the country from diverse backgrounds who he felt deserved and were well qualified for positions. Historians refer to this era as the Federalist "Fitness Test" Era because one had to show "Fitness of Character." During President Thomas Jefferson's administration (1801-1809), a political appointee's politics became an important factor in his qualifications. During President Jefferson's (a Democrat-Republican) first term, he found that "federalists" held most government jobs. Jefferson decided to balance the government workforce by appointing Democrat-Republicans until he achieved balance. He felt this would maintain the high standards and qualifications in Federal employment.

To the victor go the spoils! Very little legislation for Veterans passed prior to the Civil War. This pre-Civil War period, known as the "Spoils" Era, lasted from roughly 1832 to1883. What this meant in political terms was that every time there was a change in administration there was a massive turnover of government workers from the outgoing administration. The incoming President, his Cabinet, and the head of agencies would often delay all other business to concentrate on addressing the overzealous claims of officeseekers who came to Washington in search of political appointment. This system became the root of repaying political favors. During this time, the government began to grow and become more complex. The effects of the spoils system were becoming apparent. There was an increase in cases of malfeasance in office or outright theft by these political appointees. In one famous case, the Collector of the Port of New York could not account for $210,000 at the end of his first term. Even with the allegations President Martin Van Buren (1837-1841) reappointed him. He ended up fleeing to Europe with over $1,250,000 in public money.

We start to see congressional legislation that targets Veterans around 1861. Legislation passed granting pension benefits to Veterans with war-related disabilities and dependents of Civil War soldiers killed in action, including widows. Congress expanded the program over the next 30 years until the pension office became the largest government entity outside the Military. Towards the end of the Civil War, Congress passed legislation aimed at giving "Preference" to Veterans. The law in part read, "Persons honorably discharged from the Military or Navel service by reason of disability resulting from wounds or sickness incurred in the line of duty shall be preferred for appointments to civil offices, provided they are found to possess the business capacity necessary for the proper discharge of the duties of such offices." Under this legislation, appointments were limited to disabled Veterans who were otherwise qualified for the work of the position.

The 1865 legislation would stand as the primary preference law until the end of World War I. Several amendments to the law passed along the way. In 1871, we see the first occurrence of "suitability" requirements for Veterans seeking jobs. The amendment stated, "The President is authorized to prescribe such regulations for the admission of persons into the civil service of the United States as may best promote the efficiency thereof, and ascertain the fitness of each candidate in respect to age, health, character, knowledge, and ability for the branch of service into which he seeks to enter, and for this purpose he may employ suitable persons to conduct such inquiries, and may prescribe their duties, and establish regulations for the conduct of persons who may receive appointment in the civil service."

In 1876, a Congressional amendment gave preference for Reduction in Force (RIF) retention to Veterans, their widows, and orphans. The amendment provided, "That in making any reduction in force in any of the executive departments the head of such department shall retain those persons who may be equally qualified who have been honorably discharged from the military or naval service of the United States and the widows and orphans of deceased soldiers and sailors." The appointing officer determined the "equal qualifications" of the person being appointed.

The Civil Service Commission in 1888 gave absolute preference to all disabled Veterans over all other eligible candidates. The regulation gave the Veteran five extra points on the Civil Service Examination. So for example, if 70 is the minimum score on an exam, the Veteran would qualify with a score of 65 and placed at the top of the certification list. The next year President Harrison through Executive Order allowed reinstatement of honorably discharged Veterans who were former Federal Employees without time limit. Then in 1892, reinstatement rights were extended down to widows and orphans. This was the last significant Veterans' Preference legislation until 1919. The Census Act of 1919 saw the first major expansion of Veteran's Preference. The act granted preference to all honorably discharged Veterans, their widows, and orphans. Here is an excerpt, "That hereafter in making appointments to clerical and other positions in the executive branch of the Government, in the District of Columbia or elsewhere preference shall be given to honorably discharged soldiers, sailors, and marines, and widows of such, and to the wives of injured soldiers, sailors, and marines, who themselves are not qualified, but whose wives are qualified to hold such positions." There are two significant changes to previous legislation. The first was a service-connected disability was no longer the primary basis for Veterans' Preference. The second was it introduced the concept of preference for spouses in the appointing process.

In 1923, an Executive order added 10 points to the examination score of disabled Veterans, and added 5 points to the score on non-disabled Veterans. This order however did not include the provision to place preference eligible Veterans at the top of certification lists. Another Executive Order in 1929 resorted the provision that placed 10-point Veterans at the top of certification lists. In 1938, a Civil Service Commission regulation required all requests to pass-over a preference eligible Veteran for a non-preference eligible candidate to obtain approval by the commission. The Census Act of 1919 and the Executive Orders that followed remained the primary Federal Law for Veterans' Preference until The Veterans' Preference Act of 1944 passed congress.

Veterans' Preference, as it exists presently, originates from the Veterans' Preference Act of 1944. World War II required a never before seen mobilization effort that required millions of American citizens to put their lives on hold until after the War. Congress anticipated returning war Veterans would have extraordinary needs for employment assistance. In a congressional hearing House Representative Thomas D'Aesandro said; "This nation has trained 12,000,000 fighting men to destroy and kill. They have been taken away from schools, colleges, and jobs. Their home life has been broken up, and they have turned into tough soldiers and sailors.... The millions of men and women returning from the war fronts and camps will need jobs, money, training, hospitalization, and other assistance. They expect stability and security, so that they can start rebuilding their private lives. We must give them all that. It is the least we can do for them."

Veterans' groups played an important role pushing Congress and the President to promote the many regulations, and Executive Orders to a National Policy level. Congress and the Roosevelt Administration listened. President Roosevelt wrote, "I believe that the Federal Government, functioning in its capacity as an employer, should take the lead in assuring those who are in the armed forces that when they return special consideration will be given to them in their efforts to obtain employment. It is absolutely impossible to take millions of our young men out of their normal pursuits for the purpose of fighting to preserve the Nation, and then expect them to resume their normal activities without having any special consideration shown them."

Essentially the act consolidated the various rules, regulations, amendments, and Executive Orders, into one piece of legislation. It broadened the scope and added strength to existing Veterans' Preference rules by giving them legislative sanction. The Executive Branch could no longer affect Veterans' Preference. Any changes would now have to go through the Congress and the legislative process. The act made clear that preference was a reward for patriotic service by a grateful nation. A nation that was willing to recognize the sacrifices of its service members when peace arrives.

The Act helped ensure that veterans regain or obtain an economic status they otherwise would have attained had they not served in the Military. The Veterans Preference Act of 1944 defined to whom and under what circumstances preference to grant preference. It provided Veterans' Preference in competitive examinations, in appointments to positions in the Federal service, in reinstatement to positions, in reemployment, and in retention during reductions in force. Preference would apply to civilian positions, permanent or temporary, in all departments, agencies, bureaus, administrations, establishments, and projects of the Federal Government, and in the civil service of the District of Columbia. The law additionally provided that preference apply to positions in the classified civil service (now the competitive service), the unclassified civil service (positions excepted from the competitive service), and in any temporary or emergency establishment, agency, bureau, administration, project and department created by acts of Congress or Presidential Executive order.

In 1948, an amendment to the Act granted preference to the mothers of Veterans. The amendment gave to certain widowed, divorced, or legally separated mothers of Veterans (men and women) who died under honorable conditions while on active duty in any branch of the Armed Forces in wartime or peacetime campaigns or expeditions for which campaign badges or service medals were authorized; or

Have permanent and total service-connected disabilities that disqualify them for civil service appointments to positions along a general line of their usual occupations.

In 1952, a bill was passed granting Veterans' Preference to those honorably separated Veterans who served on active duty in any branch of the armed forces of the United States during the period beginning April 28, 1952 and ending July 1, 1955 (the period after the termination of the state of war between the United States and the Government of **Japan** during which persons could be inducted under existing law for training and service in the armed forces). The bill also extended preference to the widows and mothers of those Veterans.

The **Vietnam War** in the 1960s brought about several modifications of the Veterans' Preference Act of 1944. In 1966, legislation passed that granted peacetime preference for Vietnam-era Veterans who served on Active Duty for more than 180 consecutive days between January 31, 1955 and October 10, 1976. This legislation excluded National Guard and Reserve Service.

In 1967, a bill passed that expanded preference to all veterans who served on active duty for more than 180 days (no requirement to serve during war, campaign, or conflict) between January 31, 1955 and October 10, 1976. This expansion also did not include National Guard and Reserve Service.

The end of the Vietnam War ended in 1976. A bill passed that added restrictions on Veterans whose service begins after October 14, 1976. Post-Vietnam era Veterans, only received preference if they became disabled, or served in a declared war, a campaign, or expedition. The primus behind this legislation was the desire of the Department of Defense to build a post-Vietnam Era Draft career Military Service.

The Civil Service reform act of 1978 created preference eligibility for Veterans with a 30 percent or more disability. It also gave veterans extra protection in hiring and retention. Under this legislation, preference Veterans who retired at the rank of O4 and above would no longer receive preference.

1988, a law was passed that required the **Department of Labor** to report agencies' violations of veterans' preference and failure to list vacancies with State employment services to the **Office of Personnel Management** for enforcement.

The last piece of key legislation affecting Veterans' Preference occurred in the form of the Defense Appropriations Act of 1997. Under this legislation, Veterans received preference if they served on active duty during the **Gulf War** period (August 2, 1990 through January 2, 1992). This law also granted preference to certain service members who earned campaign medals for service in **Bosnia and Herzegovina** in support of **Operation Joint Endeavor** (November 20, 1995 through December 20, 1996) or **Operation Joint Guard** (December 20, 1996 through a date designated by the **Secretary of Defense**).

The National Defense Authorization Act of 2006 expanded the definition of a Veteran in 5 CFR 211.102(a) to include individuals who served on active duty for more than 180 consecutive days, other than for training, any part of which occurred during the period beginning September 11, 2001, and ending and ending on the date prescribed by Presidential proclamation or by saw as the last day of Operation Iraqi Freedom August 31, 2010.

What is Veterans' Preference?

"A people that values it privileges above its principles soon loses both." President Dwight D. Eisenhower

As you may have noticed in the previous chapter, the overarching theme of the rules, regulations, Executive Orders, and laws revolve around service during armed conflict. That is why the preference is given and is what makes the dates you served so important. Not all Veterans get preference. In my case, my first tour was during the early 1980's. The only armed conflict during that time was Granada. I did not go to Granada therefore I would not receive preference based on the dates I served unless I was disabled. I bring this up because I see Veterans applying for positions requesting Veterans' Preference with dates that are not eligible. I will explain more below.

So what is Veterans' Preference? You can do a Google search for Veterans Preference and get 2.5 million results. At the top of the list is FedsHireVets (http://1.usa.gov/1wUIIGg). **Feds Hire Vets** describes Veterans' Preference this way; *"Veterans' Preference gives eligible Veterans preference in appointment over many other applicants. Veterans' Preference applies, to virtually all new appointments in both the competitive service and excepted service. Veterans' Preference does not guarantee Veterans a job and it does not apply to internal agency actions such as promotions, transfers, reassignments, and reinstatements."* Huh? This is an excellent website with tons of useful information but in my opinion, it does not break down the information enough for old rotor-heads like me. If I read that just coming off the street, I would think that just because I am a Veteran I should have Veterans' Preference. This is not always true. The bottom line up front (BLUF) is that when you apply to a vacancy announcement where all US Citizens are eligible to apply, if you are deemed to have Veterans' Preference, and if you are qualified for the position, you will be put at the top of the Certificate/Referral list that is generated for the Selecting Official/Hiring Manager to make his/her selections for the position they have open. . The Selecting Official/Hiring Manager must select you or other preference eligible candidates before non-preference eligible candidates.

If you do not have a human resources background with the government, do you know the difference between competitive and excepted service? The words "all new appointments" are significant also. When you are applying to jobs on the USA Jobs website, how do you know these are "new" jobs? I have seen many Veterans apply to jobs that are not new. They are internal and therefore they do not meet the "area of consideration." This can be very frustrating. I will try to clear some that up in the next chapter. For now, I want to cover a few definitions in detail to give you a solid footing as to where you are and what your status is.

Did you know it is possible to be a Veteran and not meet the definition of a Veteran for the purposes of Veterans' Preference as stated in the CFR? Huh? That's right! The Code of Federal Regulations (CFR) is the law codified. It is the code or law the Office of Personnel Management (OPM) uses to authorize government agencies to hire you. When I refer to the CFR, I am referring to 5CFR-Title-5—Administrative Personnel (http://bit.ly/1Iolmje) that governs Federal Hiring.

The Office of Personnel Management (OPM) administers entitlement to Veterans' Preference in employment under title 5, United States Code, and oversees other statutory employment requirements in titles 5 and 38. Title 38 also governs Veterans' entitlements to *benefits* administered by the Department of Veterans Affairs (VA) (http://va.gov). Title 5 and 38 use many of the same terms. Unfortunately, they do not always mean the same thing. An example is service during a "war" is used for Veterans' Preference and service credit under title 5. OPM interprets this to mean a war declared by congress . In title 38, "period of war" includes many non-declared wars such as the Persian Gulf War, the Korean War, and the Vietnam War. These conflicts entitle Veterans to VA benefits under Title 38 but not necessarily Veterans' Preference under Title 5.

The first thing we have to figure out is do you meet the Title 5 definition of a Veteran. For the purposes of Veterans' Preference in Federal employment, the following definitions apply. These come directly from the CFR. I have added explanatory notes in parentheses and italics.

(a) Veteran means a person who has been discharged or released from active duty in the Armed Forces under honorable conditions performed —

(1) In a war; **OR**, *(a War has to be declared like World War II) (also notice the word "or" behind each sentence)*

(2) In a campaign or expedition for which a campaign badge has been authorized; **OR** *(you must have been awarded the badge or medal, example the Iraqi Campaign Medal or an Armed Forces Expeditionary Medal and it must appear on your DD214)*

(3) During the period beginning April 28, 1952, and ending July 1, 1955; **OR**

(4) For more than 180 consecutive days, <u>other than for training</u>, any part of which occurred during the period beginning February 1, 1955, and ending October 14, 1976; **OR** *(other than for training is very important here)*

(5) During the period beginning August 2, 1990, and ending January 2, 1992; **OR**

(6) For more than 180 consecutive days, <u>other than for training</u>, any part of which occurred during the period beginning September 11, 2001, and ending on August 31, 2010. The date prescribed by Presidential proclamation or by law as the last day of Operation

Iraqi Freedom. *("Other than for training" is very important here. If you are a member of the National Guard or a Reserve Component and only went to basic training and AIT, Tech School, A School, etc., you are not eligible for Veterans Preference unless you have a service connected disability)*

(b) **Disabled Veteran** means a person who has been discharged or released from active duty in the armed forces under honorable conditions performed at any time and who has established the present existence of a service-connected disability or is receiving compensation, disability retirement benefits, or pension because of a statute administered by the Department of Veterans Affairs or a military department.

(c) Preference Eligible means veterans, spouses, widows, or mothers who meet the definition of "preference eligible" in 5 U.S.C. 2108 (http://bit.ly/1DpHcP4). Preference eligibles are entitled to have 5 or 10 points added to their earned score on a civil service examination (see 5 U.S.C. 3309 {http://bit.ly/1CEsRiD}). They are also accorded a higher retention standing in the event of a reduction in force (see 5 U.S.C. 3502 {http://bit.ly/1CEt19G}). Preference does not apply, however, to in-service placement actions such as promotions.

(d) Armed Forces means the United States Army, Navy, Air Force, Marine Corps, and Coast Guard.

(e) Uniformed Services means the armed forces, the commissioned corps of the Public Health Service, and the commissioned corps of the National Oceanic and Atmospheric Administration.

(f) **Active duty or active military duty**

(1) Active Duty or Active Duty Military for veterans defined in paragraphs (a) (1) through (3) and disabled veterans defined in paragraph (b) above means active duty with military pay and allowances in the armed forces, including training or for determining physical fitness and including service in the Reserves or National Guard.

(2) **Active duty or active military duty** for a veteran defined in paragraph (a)(4) through (6) of this section means full-time duty with military pay and allowances in the armed forces, except for training or for determining physical fitness and except for service in the Reserves or National Guard.

(g☐Discharged or Released from Active Duty means with either an honorable or a general discharge from active duty in the armed forces. The Department of Defense is responsible for administering and defining military discharges.

When does Veterans' Preference Apply?

"People sleep peaceably in their bed at night only because rough men stand ready to do violence on their behalf" Gorge Orwell

All of the preceding pages of this book have led us to this chapter. Now that we know where Veterans' Preference came from and why we are afforded preference, now we can learn how to apply it. I am going to follow the outline of the OPM Vet Guide (http://1.usa.gov/16RZ8p9). I will add comments and explanations where applicable.

Veterans' Preference in hiring applies to permanent and temporary positions in the Competitive (http://1.usa.gov/1CEtj0g) and Excepted (http://1.usa.gov/1zik0fc) services of the executive branch. What executive branch means is it applies to any position in any department that has a direct line of reporting to the President. It applies basically, to any department with a Cabinet Secretary, for example, the Department of Defense, The Department of Commerce, and the Department of Agriculture. It does not apply to Senior Executive Service positions like the Director for OPM or to executive branch positions that require Senate confirmations. The judicial and legislative are also exempt from Veterans' Preference unless the positions are in the competitive service or covered by another law.

The OPM Vet Guide says, "Preference applies in hiring from civil service examinations conducted by the Office of Personnel Management (OPM) and agencies under delegated examining authority, for most excepted service jobs including Veterans Recruitment Appointments (VRA), and when agencies make temporary, term, and overseas limited appointments. Veterans' preference does not apply to promotion, reassignment, transfer, reinstatement, and change to lower grade". Wow that was a mouthful. The term "civil service examinations" makes me think of taking a test like the SAT, ACT or ASVAB or the Postal Exam. That term can be misleading. I did a simple Google search for "Civil Service Exam" and got 11 million results. The first page results are for state and local hiring authorities or for bait and switch websites. I didn't check all 11 million but I didn't see anything official about federal civil service exams on the first couple pages. Don't be tempted to buy the "sample tests" and "study guides". Do your research. You see in most cases the "examination" in federal hiring is the application. There is no longer a single civil service exam for all government jobs. Your knowledge, skills, and abilities are "examined" during the application process by the assessment questionnaire, resume, or other items required by most vacancy announcements. Testing, if any, is dependent upon the agency and position.

Veterans' preference does not require an agency to use any particular appointment process. Agencies have broad authority under law to hire from any appropriate source of eligible candidates including those claiming special appointing authorities like VRA, VEOA etc. The agency you are applying to may consider candidates already in the civil service from an agency-developed merit promotion list or it may reassign a current employee, transfer an employee from another agency, or reinstate a former Federal employee. In addition, agencies are required to give priority to displaced employees before using civil service examinations and similar hiring methods.

Types of Veterans' Preference

"The Soldier is the Army. No Army is better than its Soldiers. The Soldier is also a citizen. In fact, the highest obligation and privilege of citizenship is that of bearing arms for one's country" George S Patton Jr.

As stated in the preceding chapter, to receive preference a Veteran must have been discharged or released from active duty in the Armed Forces under honorable conditions. We also know that Armed Forces also means service in the Army, Navy, Air Force, Marine Crops, or Coast Guard. You must also be eligible for one of the preference types below. The acronyms, TP, CP, CPS, XP, are internal shorthand OPM uses in competitive examinations. I have not been able to nail down what the letters actually stand for. You will hear that TP stands for "Tentative Preference" or CP stands for "Compensable Preference" but I have not been able to find a reference anywhere in policy or regulation. For the purposes of adjudicating Veterans Preference just know that when you see these acronyms they correspond to the definitions below.

Keep in mind that if you retired at the rank of Major, Lieutenant Commander, or higher you are not eligible for Veterans Preference unless you are disabled. This does not apply to Reservists who will not begin drawing military retired pay until age 60. For example, if you are an O4 or above and are serving in or retiring from a Reserve component (including National Guard) of the Armed Forces, and you received an Honorable Discharge from a deployment to Afghanistan, you would NOT qualify for Veterans Preference unless you were disabled.

This applies to all. If you are a disabled Veteran you should also use the **Standard Form (SF) 15** (http://1.usa.gov/1xgig4Z) to help you define your preference eligibility. Most agencies require it in your application and actually provide a link in the Vacancy Announcement.

Read the form thoroughly front and back. It has definitions and will tell you what required documents you must upload with your application. If you are not disabled, and you served or are serving in a Reserve component of the Armed Forces, "active duty for training" does not qualify for Veterans' Preference. But if you were injured during that training and are receiving compensation for that injury, you would qualify for Veterans Preference.

When you apply for Federal jobs, you should claim the preference on your application and also state it in your resume. In a later chapter, Applying Veterans' Preference in USA JOBS, I will show you how to do this. The bottom line here is in most agencies if you don't claim it you won't get it and if you don't support it you won't get it. Again, don't leave it up to the Human Resources Specialist to assume you have preference. The fact that you attached a DD 214 does not guarantee you preference you have to claim it and be eligible. I know it sounds silly but take my word for it.

The preference categories below and point values are based on 5 U.S.C. 2108 and 5 U.S.C. 3309. Remember that agencies can differ on how they apply Veterans' Preference so the term "points" can have different meaning from agency to agency. Some agencies "Rack and Stack" preference eligible candidates. That means they put them in order within the preference category. For example you have a list of candidates where you have Veterans who are eligible for TP, CP, and CPS. When the Certificate/Referral list is issued to the Selecting Official/Hiring Manager, CPS candidates will be on top, then the CP, then the TP based on the category, i.e. CPS=30% or more, CP=0 to 29%, and TP=not disabled. In most cases that is the order the position will be offered. The following applies to active duty time served other than for training, in a Regular component of the Armed Forces or if you were called to active duty by order of the President in a Reserve Component including the National Guard.

5-Point Preference (TP) — to receive TP preference you must have served:

> During a War (WWII Veterans); OR
>
> During the period April 28, 1952 through July 1, 1955 (Most Korea War Veterans); OR
>
> For more than 180 consecutive days, other than for training, any part of which occurred after January 31, 1955 and before October 15, 1976 (most Vietnam Veterans); OR
>
> During the Gulf War from August 2, 1990, through January 2, 1992 (see note 1 below); OR
>
> For more than 180 consecutive days, other than for training, any part of which occurred during the period beginning September 11, 2001 and ending August 31, 2010 the official end of Operation Iraqi Freedom. (Post 9/11 Veterans); OR
>
> In a campaign or expedition for which a campaign medal is authorized. Any Armed Forces Expeditionary Medal or campaign badge, including El Salvador, Lebanon, Grenada, Panama, Southwest Asia, Somalia, and Haiti, qualified for preference. (See note 2 below)

Note 1: If you are a campaign medal holder or Gulf War Veteran who originally enlisted after September 7, 1980 or began active duty after October 14, 1982 you must have completed 24 months of continuous active duty before, during, or after August 2, 1990 through January 2, 1992 or the full period you were called to active duty if you were in a Reserve Component. There is also some information specific to Gulf War Veterans in the OPM Vet Guide under the heading A word about Gulf War Veterans.

Note 2: If you received a campaign badge or expeditionary medal IT MUST show on your DD214 or DD215

The following applies to Veterans who have a compensable disability rating. A compensable disability is one in which the Department of Veteran Affairs (VA) has determined is service-connected and meets the scheduler requirements for a compensable evaluation according to Title 38-Chapter 1-Part 4 (http://bit.ly/1zZcD36). The easiest way to explain the term "compensable" is that it is a VA compensation benefit paid on the basis the kind and severity of a disability that happened as a result of your active duty military service. In other words you must be receiving payment from the VA for a service connected disability. Go to the Veterans Benefits Administration (http://benefits.va.gov/benefits/) web site and click on the applicable links for all current information about compensation and pension, eligibility, payment rates, application, etc.

10-Point Compensable Disability Preference (CP) — to receive this preference you must have served:

> At any time and have a compensable service-connected disability rating of 10 percent but less than 30 percent.

10-Point Compensable Disability Preference (CPS) — to receive this preference you must have served:

> At any time and have a compensable service connected disability rating of 30 percent or more. The following applies to Veterans who have a non-compensable disability. A non-compensable disability is one which the VA has determined is service connected, but does not meet the scheduler requirements for compensable evaluation.

10-Point Disability Preference (XP) — to receive this preference you must have served:

> At any time and have a present service connected disability or be receiving compensation, disability,

retirement benefits, r pension from the military or the Department of Veterans Affairs but does not qualify for CP or CPS; OR

Be a Veteran who received a Purple Heart

The following applies to spouses, widows, widowers, and mothers of Veterans. This "Derived Preference" relies on the premise that the Veteran is unable to use the preference they are eligible for based on their service. The mother and spouse (including widow and widower) may both be entitled to Veterans' Preference at the same time. However, if the Veteran is living **AND** eligible for Federal Employment, neither will be eligible for preference. I will explain more below.

10 Point Derived Preference (XP) Spouse—to receive this preference you must be the spouse of a disabled Veteran who is **disqualified** for a Federal position along the lines of his or her usual occupation **because of a service connected disability**. For example, if the Veteran is a diesel engine mechanic by trade, it was their normal job, and because of a service connected disability he/she was unable to perform the duties of that position, the Veteran would be disqualified from having a diesel mechanic's job in the Federal Government. Therefore the Spouse of the Veteran would be able to use the preference the Veteran was otherwise eligible for. Such a disqualification may be presumed **when the Veteran is unemployed AND;**

> Is rated by appropriate Military or Department of Veterans Affairs authorities to be 100 percent disabled and/or unemployable: OR
>
> Has retired, been separated, or resigned from a civil service position on the basis of a disability that is service connected in origin; OR
>
> Has attempted to obtain a civil service position or other position along the lines of his or her usual occupation and has failed to qualify because of a service-connected

disability.

Spousal preference may be given under different circumstances but it must rise to the level above. Anything less would be looked at very carefully.

It is also important to note that this spousal preference is different from the preference the Department of Defense is required by law to extend to spouses of active duty members in filling its civilian positions. Military One Source (http://www.militaryonesource.mil/) has a page devoted to Military Spouse Preference in Employment.

10-Point Derived Preference (XP) Widow/Widower — to receive this preference the widow or widower of a Veteran must not been divorced from the Veteran, has not remarried, or the remarriage was annulled, and the Veteran either:

> Served during a war or during the period April 28, 1952 through July 1, 1955, or in a campaign or expedition for which a campaign medal has been authorized; OR

> Died while on active duty that included service described immediately above under conditions that would not have been the basis for other than honorable or general discharge.

10-Point Derived Preference (XP) Mother of a decease Veteran — to receive this preference a person must be the mother of a Veteran who died under honorable conditions while on active duty during a war or during the period April 28, 1952 through July 1, 1955, or in a campaign or expedition for which a campaign medal has been authorized; AND

> She is or was married to the father of the Veteran; AND

> She lives with her totally and permanently disabled husband (either the Veteran's father or her husband through remarriage); OR

> She is widowed, divorced, or separated from the Veteran's father and is not remarried; OR

> separated from her husband when she claims preference.

10-Point Derived Preference (XP) Mother of a disabled Veteran—to receive this preference a person must be the mother of a living disabled Veteran if the Veteran was separated with an honorable or general discharge from active duty, including training service in the Reserves or National Guard, performed at any time AND is permanently disabled form a service connected injury or illness; and the mother:
Is or was married to the father of the Veteran; AND

> Lived with her totally and permanently disabled husband (either the Veteran's father or her husband through remarriage); OR
> Is widowed, divorced, or separated from the Veteran's father and has not remarried; OR
> Remarried but is widowed, divorced or legally separated from her husband when she claims the preference.

As you can see the over-arching tone of the mother of a deceased or disabled Veteran is that the mother is not married or that her husband cannot work because of a disability. Therefore she would be the sole bread winner either for herself, the totally disabled Veteran, or her husbandless, fatherless family. I know that may sound sexist in this day and age but think about when this law was written; post WWII.

Special Hiring Authorities for Veterans

"There is no secret to success. It is the result of preparation, hard work, and learning from failure" Colin Powell

In the previous chapter we discussed Veterans' Preference as it pertains to competitive hiring. Remember competitive hiring is just what it sounds like. To get a competitive service job you must compete against other preference and non-preference eligible candidates in open competition for a position. Now we will discuss non-competitive hiring in the Federal Government as it pertains to Veterans. Non-competitive hiring also means exactly what it sounds like. You don't have to compete against other candidates in open competition. The 30% Disabled Veterans Appointing Authority, the Veterans Employment Opportunity Authority (VEOA) and the Veterans Recruitment Appointment Authority (VRA) are three primary means to get hired non-competitively as a Veteran.

How do I apply non-competitively to a Vacancy Announcement? Keep in mind that agencies have a large number of hiring authorities to choose from when filling a vacancy. Read the USA Jobs vacancy announcement thoroughly. In many instances the announcement will encourage Veterans to apply but the agency is not <u>required</u> to hire a Veteran. Hiring in Federal agencies differs in many ways. The bottom line with non-competitive hiring is to get your resume and credentials in front of a Selecting Official. There a couple of ways to do that. One is to always apply competitively to a position you think you are qualified for.

During the application process you will be asked about your non-competitive eligibility (I will cover this in a later chapter). This will let the Human Resources Specialist and the Selecting Official know you are eligible for non-competitive hiring. Another way is to contact the Selecting Official directly. How do I do that? Every Vacancy Announcement in USA Jobs has an agency point of contact. They usually list their telephone number and email address. You can imagine that the selecting official will get a multitude of inquiries about the position so don't be offended if he/she does not respond right away. If the position is local for you, you can actually hand carry your resume and give it directly to the Selecting Official. Again don't be offended if they don't have time to sit and chat. Another way is if you know someone at the agency. Federal Employees can make recommendations for hiring people they know as long as it doesn't violate any of the prohibited personnel practices.

Why would a Selecting Official hire someone non-competitively? Usually it is because the process is many times faster to hire a non-competitive candidate versus a competitive. Earlier I mentioned the OPM 80 day hiring model. The operative word is "model". It is a goal that agencies shoot for. Some make it, some don't. All the Selecting Official knows is that there is a vacancy on his/her team. They want to fill that vacancy as soon as possible. Consider this. What happened when a member of your team was sick or injured or had a changed in duty station? The amount of work doesn't change right? Other team members including you would have to pitch in to make up the deficit. Selecting Officials are the same. Taking on extra work detracts from accomplishing their own assigned work. A non-competitive hire is the fastest way to fill a Vacancy other than some sort or Critical hiring authority.

Veterans Recruitment Authority (VRA)

Government Agencies, if they choose to, can use the VRA as a special hiring authority to hire Veterans without competition to positions at any grade level up through GS-11 or the equivalent. The promotion potential for the position does not matter. For example, if the position you are applying to is a Career Ladder GS-11/12/13, you can still be hired at the GS-11 level. There is no limitation to the number of VRA appointments an individual can have during a career provided they are otherwise qualified.

If an agency has more than one VRA eligible candidate the agency must follow the procedures outlines in 5 CFR Part 302 (http://bit.ly/1CxKAbl) for making VRA appointments. This CFR Part basically says the agency must use the competitive scoring method just as if you were to have applied through the vacancy announcement. It says they must consider CPS, CP, XP, and TP in that order.

You must also complete a two year probationary period. After two years of satisfactory employment, the agency has to convert the Veteran to a career or career conditional appointment as appropriate.

Eligibility Criteria:

In 2002 Congress passed the Jobs for Veterans Act, Public Law 107-288 which made significant changes to the existing VRA eligibility criteria. To be eligible a Veteran must be;

1. A disabled Veteran; OR

2. A Veteran who served on active duty in the Armed Forces during a War or Campaign or expedition for which a campaign badge has been authorized; OR

3. A Veteran who, while serving on active duty in the Armed Forces, participated in a United States military operation for which an Armed Forces Service Medal (http://bit.ly/1LPQS8Y) was awarded; OR

4. Recently separated Veterans (with the last 3 years)

If you are claiming eligibility under VRA you must have been separated under Honorable conditions. Additionally if you are claiming eligibility based on a campaign badge or expeditionary medal you must be in receipt of the campaign badge or medal.

Note: Under VRA eligibility criteria, not all 5-point preference eligible Veterans are eligible for VRA and vice versa.

Example 1. A veteran who served during Vietnam for more than 180 consecutive days after January 31, 1955, and before October 15, 1976 but did not receive a service connected disability or an Armed Forces Service Medal or campaign badge or expeditionary medal would be entitled to a 5-Point (TP) Preference but would not be eligible for VRA.

Example 2 A Veteran who served after August 31, 2010 and did not received a but did not receive a service connected disability or an Armed Forces Service Medal or campaign badge or expeditionary medal would NOT be eligible for 5-Point (TP) preference but if they received an Global War on Terrorism (GWOT) Service Medal, they ARE eligible for VRA.

30 Percent or More Disabled Veterans

Agencies may give a non-competitive temporary appointment of more than 60 days or a term appointment to any Veteran who:

1. Retired from active military service with a disability rating of 30 percent or more; OR

2. Has been rated by the Department of Veterans Affairs after 1991 including disability determinations from a branch of the Armed Forces at any time, as having a service-connected disability of 30 percent or more.

There is no grade limit to this appointment and the agency may convert without a break in service to a career or career conditional appointment at any time during your temporary or term appointment.

Veterans Employment Opportunities Act of 1998 (VEOA)

The Veterans Employment Opportunities Act (VEOA) of 1998 was amended by Section 511 of the Veterans Millennium Health Care Act (Pub. Law 106-117) of November 30, 1999, and it says that agencies must allow preference eligible candidates or eligible veterans to apply for positions announced under merit promotion procedures (internal vacancy announcements) when the agency is recruiting from outside its own workforce.

Eligibility Requirements; to be eligible for a VEOA appointment, an applicant must:

Be a preference eligible OR veteran separated from the armed forces after 3 or more years of continuous active service performed under honorable conditions. Veterans who were released shortly before completing a 3-year tour are considered to be eligible. ("Active service" defined in title 37, United States Code, means active duty in the uniformed services and includes full-time training duty, annual training duty, full-time National Guard duty, and attendance, while in the active service, at a school designated as a service school by law or by the Secretary of the military department concerned).

What to Look For on Your DD Form 214

"I can imagine no more rewarding a career. And any man who may be asked in this century what he did to make his life worthwhile, I think can respond with a good deal of pride and satisfaction: 'I served in the United States Navy"—John F. Kennedy

The DD 214 is the most important document you will ever receive in regards to your military service. I cannot stress enough how important it is to safeguard it. As soon as you separate or, if you haven't done it already, go to your county or parish clerk of courts office and register your Member 4 Copy. It is a very simple process. They make a copy of it, stamp it with the county seal and file it away for safekeeping. That way there will always be a copy available if you need it. Additionally scan the document and put it on a thumb drive and put it in a fire proof safe. If you have a safety deposit box at a bank, get someone to notarize a copy for you and put it in there. Better still put the original in the safety deposit box and keep the notarized version at home. Anything you can do to protect this document you should do. I know it may seem a bit over the top but if you ever have to request a copy from the National Archives (http://www.archives.gov/) you will thank me.

In this chapter I use redacted sections of my own DD Form 214 and others I have found on the web to use as examples illustrating the important parts of the from. I do not keep any of the personally identifiable information (PII) I find. Notice I said "I find". I did a Google image search and got back thousands of examples of real DD 214's, which was somewhat troubling. Some of the results even have social security numbers on them. Protect yourself from identity theft folks.

There are many versions of this form. There have even been changes even since I retired in 2006. Yours may not look exactly like the examples in this chapter. The information I am showing you is somewhere on all the different versions. You just may have to look around for it especially those prior to the early 1970's

What is a DD214?

Simply put the Department of Defense Form 214 (DD214) is a document the Department of Defense issues to service members who retire, separate or discharge from active Military duty. The very first DD214 was issued in 1950 replacing the War Department Adjutant General's Office (WD AGO) and the Navy Personal (NAVPERS) discharge documents from World War II. Your DD214 is your statement of service.

There is an old saying, *"If it is not listed on your DD214 then it didn't happen."* This document represents the verified record of your active and/or inactive service in the Military, your awards and decorations, date of rank, Military training/schooling, combat service, overseas service, and your Military occupational specialty. Additionally it contains other pertinent service information such as codes used by the Armed forces to describe your reason for discharge and reenlistment eligibility. These codes are known as Separation Designator/Separation Justification (SPD/SJC) Codes and Reenlistment Eligibility (RE) Codes.

What is the DD214 used for?

The DD214 is used by the Department of Veterans Affairs and other government agencies to secure Veteran Benefits and may be requested by employers especially if the company is dealing with DOD contracts or other classified/sensitive information. It is usually required by funeral directors to immediately prove eligibility for interment in a VA/National Cemetery. It is also used for obtaining a Veteran's grave marker and/or Military Honors for a deceased Veteran. The Defense Authorization Act of 2000 allowed at the family's request, every eligible Veteran to receive a military funeral honors ceremony to include the folding and presentation of the United States burial flag and the sounding of Taps at no cost to the family.

Why are there so many Copies?

There are 8 copies of your DD214. These copies are distributed to various locations. The most important copy is the Member 4 copy. This is the standard form used by government agencies such as the VA to verify that you are eligible for Benefits such as the GI Bill or Veterans Preference. The 8 copies are distributed and described below

1. Copy 1—this copy is given to the service member. I have read somewhere that this copy may have been deleted but I have not been able to confirm. At any rate in my opinion it virtually worthless it does not have your character of service. You cannot be given Veterans Preference for Federal Hiring with a Member 1 copy. The Human Resources Specialist must see your character of service. The Member 1 copy is known as the short form because the additional Information blocks at the

bottom are left off.

2. Copy 2—Remains with your Service Personnel File

3. Copy 3—this copy is sent to the United States Department of Veterans Affairs.

4. Copy 4—this copy is given to the service member and should be safe guarded.

5. Copy 5—this copy is sent to the United States Department of Labor.

6. Copy 6—this copy is sent to the State Director of Veteran Affairs.

7. Copy 7 & 8—are distributed in accordance with the appropriate Military Service directives (either shredded or retained.)

IMPORTANT NOTE: NEVER EVER, EVER NEVER, NEVER, NEVER (get my point?) submit your Member 1 copy when you apply to a federal job. It will do you no good. It does not have your character of service. That is the first thing a Humana Resources Specialist is going to look for. You will almost certainly NOT be given Veteran's Preference unless you accompany it with a disability letter from the VA.

It is important to note that any of the other copies EXCEPT for Member Copy 1 can be used to verify Veterans Preference for hiring within the Federal Government because they all have the same information. Policies differ from agency to agency so you best bet is to submit your Member 4 Copy as a rule. If you have lost your member 4 copy and have another copy that shows the character of service, you can still submit it for review. You may get push back from the HR Specialist. If you get push back or if you do not get Veterans Preference when you know you are eligible, as for a second level review. Nowhere in the OPM Vet Guide does it stipulate that you must have a Member Copy 4. It only state you have an Honorable discharge.

Important sections of you DD214

     As I stated earlier the DD214 has been around since 1950. It has undergone several changes and overhauls over the years. I will highlight the most common areas that Human Resources Specialists look for when reviewing your DD214 for Veterans Preference.

     Blocks 1 through 6 of the DD214 is where most of your Personally Identifiable Information is. The information the Human Resources Specialist looks for here is the Grade or Rank. Remember if you retired at the rank of Major, Lieutenant Commander, or higher you are not eligible for Veterans Preference unless you are disabled. This does not apply to Reservists who will not begin drawing military retired pay until age 60. For example, if you are an O4 or above and are serving in or retiring from a Reserve component (including National Guard) of the Armed Forces, and you received an Honorable Discharge from a deployment to Afghanistan, you would qualify for Veterans Preference even if you are not disabled.

CERTIFICATE OF RELEASE OR DISCHARGE FROM ACTIVE DUTY			
1. NAME (Last, First, Middle)	2. DEPARTMENT, COMPONENT AND BRANCH ARMY USAR		3. SOCIAL SECURITY NUMBER
4a. GRADE, RATE OR RANK SFC	b. PAY GRADE E07	5. DATE OF BIRTH (YYYYMMDD)	6. RESERVE OBLIGATION TERMINATION DATE (YYYYMMDD) 00000000

     Block 12. Record of Service is a very important sections that Human Resources Specialists look at. This section give us your dates of service data. Remember in some cases you must have served between certain dates and in some cases you must have served at least 180 consecutive days. What we look for here is the "Net Active Service This Period" block c. It is important to note you can only be given preference for the DD214 you submit. There are almost as many scenarios as there are Veterans but here is an example. A Veteran submits DD214

that has 3 years of active service on it from 1995 to 1998. Before this 3 years of Active duty the Veteran was a Reservist. The Veteran's Unit was activated and sent to Iraq. The Veteran submitted their most recent DD214 with the 3 years of active service in block 12 c. Block 12 d contains the Total <u>Prior</u> Active Service and that says 1 year. The DD214 that has the preference eligibility is the one from when the Veteran was in Iraq not from the 3 years of service. As you can see from the example the DD214 would only state the number of years and months of service not where it took place. I will continue this example in the next section.

12. RECORD OF SERVICE	YEAR(S)	MONTH(S)	DAY(S)
a. DATE ENTERED AD THIS PERIOD	2002	08	31
b. SEPARATION DATE THIS PERIOD	2006	06	30
c. NET ACTIVE SERVICE THIS PERIOD	0003	10	00
d. TOTAL PRIOR ACTIVE SERVICE	0016	02	14
e. TOTAL PRIOR INACTIVE SERVICE	0001	07	21
f. FOREIGN SERVICE	0000	00	00
g. SEA SERVICE	0000	00	00
h. EFFECTIVE DATE OF PAY GRADE	1995	10	01

Section 13. Decorations, Medals, Badges, Citations and Campaign Ribbons Awarded or Authorized is also very important. The highlighted areas below are what would give this marine his Veteran's Preference. The Iraq Campaign Medal and he Global War on Terrorism Expeditionary Medal are qualifying for Veterans' Preference. If you received these type of awards make sure they are on your DD214. If they are not you must submit for a DD215 corrected DD215.

```
┌────────────────────────────────────────────────┐
│ 13. DECORATIONS, MEDALS, BADGES, CITATIONS AND CAMPAIGN │
│     RIBBONS AWARDED OR AUTHORIZED (All periods of service) │
│ Navy and Marine Corps Achievement Medal, Marine Corps Good │
│ Conduct Medal, Iraq Campaign Medal, Sea Service Deployment │
│ Ribbon (w/1 Bronze Service Star), Global War on Terrorism │
│ Service Medal, Global War on Terrorism Expeditionary Medal │
│ (Iraq), National Defense Service Medal, Navy Unit │
│ Commendation, Letter of Appreciation, Certificate of │
└────────────────────────────────────────────────┘
```

The special additional information section is what get look at next. This is the most important section. The reason is that Veterans' Preference starts here. The very first thing a Human Resources Specialist looks for is your character of service in block 24. I have seen many different things in this box. What you MUST have is an honorable discharge. What does that mean? If I was forced out for disciplinary reasons does that count? The short Human Resources answer is "well it depends". Here are some of the Honorable Service codes I have seen. There may be others but these are the most common.

1. Honorable
2. General
3. General Under Honorable
4. N/A (This is usually used when a member has not completed a service school.

SPECIAL ADDITIONAL INFORMATION (For use by authorized agencies only)		
23. TYPE OF SEPARATION	24. CHARACTER OF SERVICE (Include upgrades)	
RETIREMENT	HONORABLE	
25. SEPARATION AUTHORITY	26. SEPARATION CODE	27. REENTRY CODE
AR 635-200, CHAP 12	RBD	4R
28. NARRATIVE REASON FOR SEPARATION		
SUFFICIENT SERVICE FOR RETIREMENT		
29. DATES OF TIME LOST DURING THIS PERIOD (YYYYMMDD)		30. MEMBER REQUESTS COPY 4 (initials)
NONE		
DD FORM 214-AUTOMATED, FEB 2000 PREVIOUS EDITION IS OBSOLETE GENERATED BY TRANSPROC		MEMBER - 4

Here are some of the less than honorable codes I have seen.

Again there may be others but these are the most common.

1. Dishonorable
2. Under Other than Honorable
3. General less than honorable.

Everyone makes mistakes. The important thing is, what you have done since. If you received an "Other than Honorable" discharge you can still be hired. You will just not receive Veterans' Preference.

Navigating USA Jobs

"America's finest — our men and women in uniform, are a force for good throughout the word, and that is nothing to apologize for."—Sarah Palin

What is **USAJobs (https://www.usajobs.gov/)**? If you have never applied for Federal employment, you probably have never heard of it. USAJobs is the U.S. Government's official system/program for Federal jobs and employment information. USAJobs delivers a service by which Federal agencies meet their legal obligation under Title 5 USC 3327 and Title 5 USC 3330 to provide public notice of Federal employment opportunities to Federal employees and U.S. citizens. The website is operated and maintained by the United States Office of Personnel Management (OPM). What this means is that this is the place where the majority of US Government Agencies post their vacancies. There are thousands of jobs available. What you have to do is sift through and find the right one for you.

One of the mistakes I made when I started applying to federal jobs is that I didn't take time to read all the information that was available to me. I just jumped in and applied to everything. There are many helpful links within USAJOBS. Before you begin I suggest reading through some of these. A good place to start is the **Resource Center (http://1.usa.gov/1CxKdgV)**. There are also links for Veterans, persons with disabilities, and students within this navigation link.

I am going to assume you created a USAJobs account. You now have to complete your profile. The information you put in your profile is transferred to each agency you apply to. Not all government agencies us the same applicant intake software. Some use Monster.com, or USA Staffing, or eRecruit etc. I am going to get your through the USAJobs side because most of the information transfers from USAJobs. I would caution here that it is your responsibility to ensure your information moves to the application from your USA Jobs Profile. You will always have one last chance to review your application before hitting the submit button. In actuality you can make changes to your application right up until the hour the announcement closes which is usually Midnight EST. on the closing date stated in the announcement.

Step 1. From the home screen click on your name in the upper right hand corner.

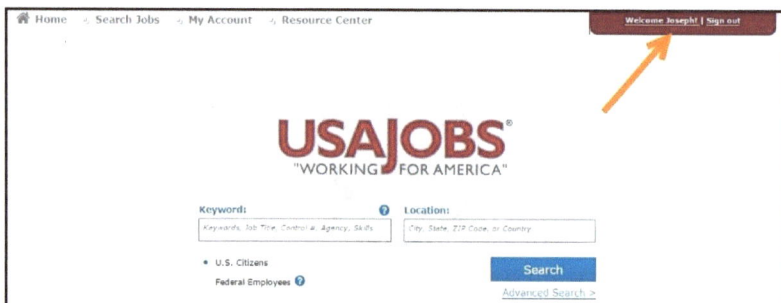

Step 2. Click on Profile

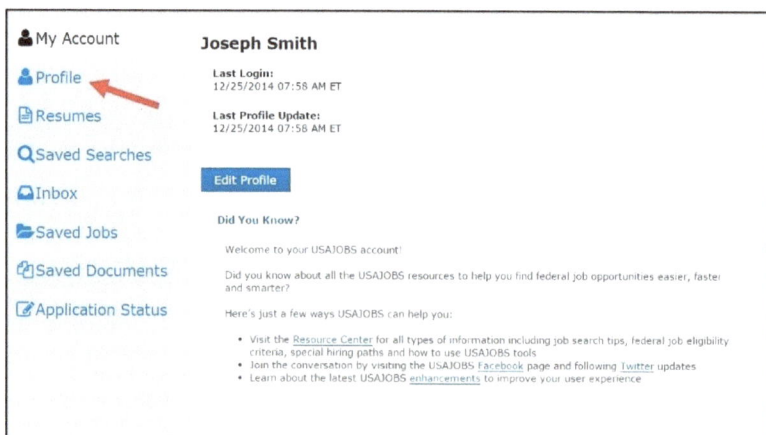

Step 3. Update your profile. The system will now walk you through updating your profile. The most important section for Veterans' Preference is hiring eligibility. First update your contact information and click next.

Step 4. Update your hiring eligibility. If you registered for selective service (which you should have even if you served) go to the **Selective Service System (http://www.sss.gov/default.htm)** and retrieve your number. Some agencies ask for this number some don't. Most will verify it with the SSS. Also if you have sons that are between 18 and 25 and they have not registered it is a good idea to register them. I registered all 4 of mine before they even had a chance to. Yea I know that's what they called me to. The Selective Service System is important for many reasons. The obvious is in case of a draft. But also if you or your sons don't register you can't get financial aid for college. The will have trouble getting a Federal Job etc. It's the Law. It's easy to forget. I deal with this all the time. The applicant has to prove to the Selective Service that they did not willfully fail to register. It is hard to prove you did not willfully do something. I forgot is not an excuse. Do them a favor and register them.

Step 5. Complete this section. Use what you learned above to make the appropriate choices.

---

3. Are you a Veteran of the U.S. Armed Forces or are you eligible for "derived" preference? *
   ● Yes   ○ No

  • Do you claim Veterans' Preference?

    ○ No, I do not claim Veterans' Preference

    ○ 0-point Sole Survivorship Preference (SSP)

    ○ 5-point preference based on active duty in the U.S. Armed Forces (TP)

    ● 10-point preference based on a compensable service connected disability of at least 10% but less than 30% (CP)

    ○ 10-point preference based on a compensable service connected disability of 30% or more (CPS)

    ○ 10-point preference for non-compensable disability or Purple Heart (XP)

    ○ 10-point preference based on widow/widower or mother of a deceased veteran, or spouse or mother of a disabled veteran (XP)

  • Are you a veteran who was separated from the armed forces under honorable conditions after completing an initial continuous tour of duty of at least 3 years (may have been released just short of 3 years)(VEOA)?
    ● Yes   ○ No

Step 6. Complete this section. If you have multiple dates of service put them all down here. If you have not been released from active duty yet you can click on the "Future/TBD Release Date" box and the end date will be grayed out.

Military Start/End Dates:

• If you are a Veteran of the U.S. Armed Forces, please indicate the start and end dates of your military service.

For military members with a separation date in the near future, please enter the Start Date and select the Future/TBD Release Date checkbox. If you have a break in service, please add your additional service dates.

Start Date	End Date	Future/TBD Release Date	
10/6/1983	3/12/1991	No	✗

Start Date:	End Date:		
10/01/2005		☑ Future/TBD Release Date	Add Date

Step 7. The Veterans' Document Upload section is the most important section of your profile besides your name and phone number. It is your responsibility to ensure your documents are uploaded, legible and correct. Most agencies will not ask for them. They will simply refer you as a non-Veteran if you are qualified for the position. The SF15 should always be filled out and attached. Not all agencies make this mandatory but some do. Always a good idea to fill out and attach it. Notice the links on each section. USAJobs is great about putting these links for additional information.

Veterans' Document Upload:

When claiming veterans' preference, preference eligibles must provide a copy of their DD 214, Certificate of Release or Discharge from Active Duty, or other acceptable documentation. Applicants claiming 10 point preference will need to submit an SF-15, Application for 10-point Veterans' Preference.

For current service members who have not yet been discharged, a certification letter of expected discharge or release from active duty within 120 days under honorable conditions is required at the time of application. Ensure your documentation reflects the character of discharge.

Veteran Document 1: DD-214 - Joseph's DD214
View | Delete   Date Uploaded: 12/25/2014

Veteran Document 2: Veteran Other - Joseph's VA Letter
View | Delete   Date Uploaded: 12/25/2014

Veteran Document 3: SF-15 - Joseph's SF15
View | Delete   Date Uploaded: 12/25/2014

Document Title: [ ]

Document Type: ❓ Select Document:
[SF-15 ▾] [Choose File] No file chosen

Files must be less than 3mb and can be in one of the following formats: GIF, JPG, JPEG, PNG, RTF, PDF, or Word (DOC or DOCX).

[Upload]   [Cancel]

The Federal Employment Status section is next and should be fill out like this if you have never been a Civilian in the Federal Service.

4. Please select the statement below which best reflects your federal employment status (if applicable). * ❓

- ⦿ I am not and have never been a federal civilian employee.
- ⃝ I am currently a federal civilian employee.
- ⃝ I am a former federal civilian employee with reinstatement eligibility.
- ⃝ I am a former federal civilian employee but do not have reinstatement eligibility.

The last section of the Hiring Eligibility sections is Special Hiring Options. If you are unsure of what you may be eligible for, click on refer to the Special Hiring Authorities chapter in this book or click on the link **Special Hiring Options (http://1.usa.gov/1yMoVWL)**. Again it is up to you to prove what you are claiming by attaching the correct supporting documentation.

Special Hiring Options ❓

Select from among the special hiring authorities listed below for which you are eligible. (Please note that agencies will require documentation of eligibility prior to your appointment.)

Identification of eligibility for any special hiring authority is entirely voluntary, and you will not be subject to any adverse treatment if you decline to provide it. If you do not wish to volunteer this information at this time, you may still choose to apply for jobs, as they are announced, under any of these special hiring authorities for which you are eligible. If you volunteer to provide information here about the special hiring authorities for which you believe you are eligible, then agencies who are searching for potential applicants to hire under one of these authorities may be able to locate your resume through USAJOBS and invite you to apply. Otherwise, this information will be retained in the USAJOBS database and not disclosed. For information on each of the special hiring options below, please review the definitions on our Special Hiring Options page.

- ☑ Veterans Recruitment Appointment (VRA)
- ☑ 30% or More Disabled Veteran
- ☐ Disabled veterans who have completed a VA training program
- ☐ Military Spouse
- ☐ Certain former overseas employees
- ☐ Schedule A Disabled

Cancel | Previous | Save | Next

Now I am going to assume you have created an account, completed your profile, selected a position you want to apply to and are ready to ensure you receive your Veterans' Preference. I did a random search for Human Resources Specialists for the entire country and I received 238 results.

I clicked on the first one

I highlighted an important piece of information when you are applying to federal positions. The "Who May Apply Section". This will tell you if you are eligible to apply to the position. You Military Service does not count as Federal Service like Civilian Service does. If you have no prior Civilian Federal Service you should only apply to jobs that sate "All US Citizens" in the "Who May Apply:" section.

Office Of The Secretary

Job Title: Human Resources Specialist (Compensation/Payroll), ZA-201-II (DEU)
Department: Department Of Commerce
Agency: Office of the Secretary
Job Announcement Number: OS/OHRM-2015-0010

SALARY RANGE:	$52,146.00 to $74,654.00 / Per Year
OPEN PERIOD:	Tuesday, December 23, 2014 to Monday, December 29, 2014
SERIES & GRADE:	ZA-0201-02
POSITION INFORMATION:	Career or Career-Conditional - Full time Permanent
PROMOTION POTENTIAL:	03
DUTY LOCATIONS:	Few vacancies in the following location(s): District of Columbia, DC View Map Washington DC, DC View Map
WHO MAY APPLY:	All qualified United States citizens
SECURITY CLEARANCE:	Not Applicable
SUPERVISORY STATUS:	No

Every announcement has a required documents section.

REQUIRED DOCUMENTS:
A complete application consists of the following:

Every required documents section has a veterans section. It will tell you exactly what you need to attach to the application to be considered as a Veteran. *IMPORTANT* If you don't have the required documentation figure out how to get it ASAP. Contact the VA or the National Archives. If you apply without the proper documents, chances are you won't be asked for them.

I see this all the time. Don't start applying until you have everything you need. You will save yourself a lot of frustration and anger.

Veterans' Preference documentation. Please indicate on your resume the type of veterans' preference you are claiming and provide the appropriate supporting documentation (DD-214 stating disposition of discharge or character of service, VA letter, SF-15, etc.) to validate your claim. For more information regarding eligibility requirements, please go to: http://www.fedshirevets.gov/job/vetpref/index.aspx

---

After you read through the announcement, click on the appropriate link to apply on line. You will now be taken to the Applicant intake software of the Agency you are applying to. There are too many and too varied to give an overview of each here. It suffices to say just read the instructions of each and you will be fine. Your USAJobs Profile should move all the information over for you. Just make sure you double check before clicking submit!

Afterword

I am going to take a few of sentences here to speak to the readers of this book who have not yet separated from the Military. As I stated at the beginning of this book. I have been where you are. I retired with 20 plus years of active duty but it took me 23 years to get there. I separated from the Military twice during that time. The first time I was young. I quickly saw the error in my ways and it was easy to get back in. The second was much different. It was nearly impossible to get back in. I was extremely lucky and was in the right place at the right time. It was a difficult period in my life, and I nearly lost everything. I only thought I was prepared to make the civilian transition.

The reality is I have never been so unprepared for anything in my life. If you have not finished your degree, if you do not have the greatest job in the world lined up, if you have not hit the lottery, if your Mommy and Daddy are not rich, if you are not barred from Reenlistment, run as fast as you can to the Retention NCO and Reenlist. It is a cruel, cruel world out here. There is no guaranteed salary or paycheck every two weeks, no free housing, no dining facility, no sick call, no paid 1.5 hour lunch breaks, no free medicine, no four weeks of leave every year. Three hots and a cot are gone! I am being overly dramatic here to make a point. Make 100% sure you are prepared to separate. When you think you are 100% prepared, check again.

One Last Thing… If you liked this book or found it helpful please leave a review for it on Amazon.com. Whether you loved it or hated it, your feedback will help us make it even better for future readers. You can review it on Amazon.com. Thank you so much!

Additionally please join our community of like-minded people at www.vetpref.com

Definitions for Common Terms Used in Vacancy Announcements

All U.S. Citizens: This means the announcement is open to anyone one in the public who wishes to apply and is a United States citizen.

Competitive Service: In the competitive service, individual must go through a competitive process (i.e. competitive examining) which is open to all applicants. This process may consist of a written test, an evaluation of the individual's education and experience, and/or an evaluation of other attributes necessary for successful performance in the position to be filled.

Excepted Service: Appointments to the Excepted Service are civil service appointments within the Federal Government that do not confer competitive status. There are a number of ways to be appointed to the excepted service such as appointed under an authority defined by the U.S. Office of Personnel Management (OPM) as excepted (e.g. Veterans Recruitment Appointment) or being appointed to a position defined by OPM as excepted (e.g. Attorneys) More information can be found about the excepted service in 5 U.S.C. 2103 and parts 213 and 302 of title 5 of the Code of Federal Regulations.

Career Appointment: Permanent appointment in the competitive service conveyed automatically after successfully completing the required term of service in a career-conditional appointment. This is typically a three year period.

Career-Conditional Appointment: Permanent appointment in the competitive service of a person who has not yet completed the required period of creditable, substantially continuous federal service.

Status, Competitive: Referring to current federal competitive service employees or former employees with competitive service reinstatement eligibility

Career Ladder Position: A position restructured to allow for entry at a lower grade level than the full performance grade level which allows for progression to the full performance level. Normally, a position is announced and filled on a competitive basis with promotion to higher grade levels made on a non-competitive basis. The career ladder refers to the range of grades to which the employee may be promoted non-competitively up to the classified full-performance level of the position. For example, a Human Resources Specialist, GS-201 position is classified at the full performance level of a GS- 12. Since this is a two-grade interval series, the career ladder position could be established at the GS-5, GS-7, GS-9, or GS-11, leading to the full performance GS-12. If the position is announced as a GS-7 target GS-12, the incumbent may be noncompetitively promoted from the GS-7, to the GS-9, to the GS-11, then to the GS-12.

Non-competitive Promotion: After having entered a career ladder, an employee may advance in grade up to the full performance level without further competition, i.e. the employee does not have to re-compete for each subsequent promotion and the agency does not have to re-announce the position in order to promote the incumbent.

Recently Separated Veteran: The United States Department of Labor defines a recently separated Veteran as a veteran separated during the three-year period beginning on the date of the veteran's discharge or release from active duty in the U.S. military.

Merit Promotion: The system under which agencies consider an employee for vacant positions on the basis of personal merit. Vacant positions are usually filled through competition with applicants (current competitive service employees) being evaluated and ranked for the position on the basis of their experience, education, competencies and performance.

Career Transition Assistance Plan: If you have never been a federal employee, you are not eligible to apply under CTAP. This program offers displaced federal employees priority for jobs within the agency from which they have separated or are separating. For more information, please visit OPM's Workforce Restructuring Career Transition page (http://1.usa.gov/1zQG1qB).

Competencies: A competency is a measurable pattern of knowledge, skills, abilities, behaviors and other characteristics that an individual needs in order to perform work roles or occupational functions successfully.

Delegated Examining: Delegated examining (external, public announcements) is a hiring authority used to fill competitive service jobs with:

1. Applicants applying from outside the federal workforce

2. Federal employees who do not have competitive service status

3. Federal employees with competitive service status

Direct Hire Authority: A hiring authority used to fill permanent or non-permanent positions in the competitive service at a GS-15 (or equivalent) and below, if OPM determines that there is either a severe shortage of candidates or a critical hiring need for such positions. Vacancies filled under this authority must be advertised via public notice; however, veterans' preference, rule of three, rating and ranking procedures do not apply (i.e., appointments may be made without regard to title 5, United States Code (U.S.C.) §§ 3309-3318).

Employment Program for People with Disabilities (Commonly known as Schedule a Hiring Authority): The federal government has a special appointing authority for persons with disabilities. If you meet the eligibility requirements listed below, you could obtain a position without competing with other applicants. To be eligible, you must meet the specific eligibility requirements to include:

1. Have a severe physical, cognitive, or emotional disability;
2. Have a history of having such disability; or
3. Be perceived as having such disability.

You must obtain a certification letter from a State Vocational Rehabilitation Office or the Department of Veterans Affairs to be eligible. For more information, please visit OPM's Excepted Service Appointing Authorities page (http://1.usa.gov/1DBRuZY).

Interagency Career Transition Assistance Plan: If you have never been a federal employee, you are not eligible to apply under ICTAP. This program offers displaced federal employees priority for jobs in federal agencies other than the agency from which they separated. For more information, please visit OPM's Workforce Restructuring Career Transition page.

Interchange Agreements: Allow certain current federal employees serving on excepted service appointments the opportunity to apply under merit promotion (internal) application procedures. For more information, please visit OPM's Hiring Authorities Competitive Hiring page.

Knowledge, Skills, and Abilities (KSAs): Are a list of special qualifications and personal attributes that you need to have for a particular job. These are the unique requirements that DHS wants to find in applicants for a job. KSAs are defined as the factors that identify the better candidates from a group of people basically qualified for a position. How well an applicant can show that he or she matches the position's defined KSAs will determine whether that person will be seriously considered for a job

Reinstatement: If you worked for the federal government and left, you may be eligible for reinstatement. If you previously held a career or career-conditional appointment in the federal government in which you completed three years of continuous creditable federal service, you may be eligible to obtain a position without applying through delegated examining procedures. There is a three-year time limit on using reinstatement eligibility if you only acquired career-conditional status (normally three years or less).

Selective Placement Factor: There are some positions where specific qualifications are absolutely required because a person cannot perform successfully in the position without such qualifications. These qualifications may include specific knowledge, skills, and abilities (KSAs) or federal or state licenses or certifications.

Specialized Experience: A description of the required knowledge, skills, and abilities (KSAs) that you must possess to perform the work of a position. DHS explains specialized experience in the qualifications section of the job announcement.

Time-in-Grade: Only applies to current federal competitive service employees applying for a job under merit promotion procedures. Generally, an employee may not be promoted more than two grades within one year to positions up to the GS-05 grade level. Above the GS-05 grade level, an employee must serve a minimum of one year in a particular grade, and cannot be promoted more than one grade or two grades, per year, if that is the normal progression. Time-in-grade requirements are intended to prevent excessively rapid promotions in the General Schedule.

Resource Links

VetPref http://www.vetpref.com/

United States Department of Veterans Affairs
http://www.va.gov/

The Office of Personnel Management http://www.opm.gov/

The OPM Vet Guide http://www.opm.gov/policy-data-oversight/veterans-services/vet-guide/

Feds Hire Vets http://www.fedshirevets.gov/index.aspx

National Archives http://www.archives.gov/veterans/

United States Department of Labor http://www.dol.gov/vets/

The VOW Act http://benefits.va.gov/VOW/education.asp

The Post 911 GI Bill
http://www.benefits.va.gov/gibill/post911_gibill.asp

List of State VA Websites
http://www.dd214.us/state_va.html

DD214 Separation Codes
http://www.dd214.us/reference/SPN_Codes.pdf

DD214 Reenlistment Codes
http://www.dd214.us/reference/Reenlistment_Codes.pdf

www.ingramcontent.com/pod-product-compliance
Lightning Source LLC
LaVergne TN
LVHW010025070426
835509LV00001B/6